NURSERY RHYMES OF SOUTH SUDAN

LEJU MOGA

RiverNile
PUBLISHING
LET ALL IDEAS WORTH SPREADING FLOW

RIVER NILE PUBLISHING

GRAND RAPIDS, MICHIGAN

![RiverNile PUBLISHING — LET ALL IDEAS WORTH SPREADING FLOW]

NURSERY RHYMES OF SOUTH SUDAN © 2019 LEJU MOGA

ISBN: 978-0-9996494-2-8

RiverNile
PUBLISHING
LET ALL IDEAS WORTH SPREADING FLOW

PREFACE

In South Sudan, singing or chanting a song is part of growing up as a child. In the villages, it is not uncommon to see a herd boy driving his herd of animals to the grazing land, while singing or whistling a song. It is also not uncommon to see a young girl grinding or pounding some grain while singing. In fact in the villages, the art of singing is part of raising up a child. For example, in many villages before a baby could even talk a mother or a caregiver has already began singing lullabies to the baby. These lullabies do not only calm a baby down or get the baby to sleep. They stimulate the baby's brain and make the baby get acquainted to the human voice. Lullabies also make the baby acquainted to the organized and meaningful chunks of sounds which we call words.

Indeed as a baby grows, the baby is introduced to some other songs which involve singing, clapping hands or tapping the foot. These children songs which are commonly referred to as nursery rhymes do not only entertain the children, they introduce children to various concepts such as counting or naming the outer parts of the body like the head, arms, legs and toes. These songs also help parents bond with their children and engage in a meaningful discussion. Apart from that, these songs enable children to participate, collaborate, and take responsibility in the activities they are assigned to do.

In the villages, nursery rhymes are not the only songs. Many stories and games in the villages of South Sudan have parts that have to be sung. This makes the stories more interesting, more involving, and more memorable to the children.

Nonetheless, today, many of these educative songs have remained oral in the villages. None of them have been adopted and brought into the nursery schools in Africa. Why? It all goes to the story of the beginning of formal education in Africa. When mission schools were introduced in Africa and South Sudan in particular, many things that had sustained generations after generations of Africans were considered backward and thrown away. And this attitude has remained in the minds of the mission school graduates in Africa. Today no one has gone to the villages to harvest the knowledge, the skills, the practices, and the content that had served Africa for as long as Africa has existed.

PREFACE

Therefore, the first purpose of writing this book is to bring back the very educative children songs that had been used for educating generations after generations of African children. The second purpose of writing this book is to inspire Africans to collect their traditional children songs before they disappear in the globalizing world where parents spend at a lot of time working in locations far away from their children and do not have the time to impart the oral knowledge that was imparted to them by their parents.

So, let us bring to our children the diverse children songs, so that they can appreciate the diverse world that they live in.

A BRIEF INTRODUCTION TO NURSERY RHYMES

WHAT ARE NURSERY RHYMES

Nursery rhymes are very pleasant children poems or songs. They have very short verses that can be sung or recited. They are good for children aged 3-6 years or more. They are children's favorite in many cultures of the world because they are composed in patterns where words or phrases are repeated in particular places within the text. Because the words or the phrases are repeated verse to verse, kids always find it easy to predict which word or phrase will follow in a verse. This prediction encourages kids to jump in to sing or read along. The repetitions also make nursery rhymes pleasing to the ear and easy to remember.

Nursery rhymes tell stories. They tell stories about people, animals, and things. Nursery rhymes tell stories with details that may be funny or even silly. Nursery rhymes details may also include onomatopoeic words. Onomatopoeic words are interesting words that mimic the sounds or the actions of the things or the animals that make the sounds and actions. For example, the word twinkle just mimics the action of a star shinning and flickering and the word meow just mimics the sound of a cat.

The authors of most of the nursery rhymes that are known today are unknown. This is because a lot of the nursery rhymes that we know today have been handed down orally from one generation to the next. Nonetheless there are other nursery rhymes with known authors.

WHAT IS RHYMING

Rhyming is the repetition of similar sounding words at the end of two or more lines of a verse of a poem or a song. The repetition of similar sounding words in a line of a verse is what creates a pattern of sounds that are pleasant to the ear. Words that rhyme include words such as lane and dame.

WHAT IS ALLITERATION

Alliteration is the repetition of consonant letters in succession in a line of a song or poems. Take for example the poetry lines; Sally sells shells by the sea shore, goose goose gander, Kuku kulo a kakuruk. In these lines there is a successive repetition of the S-sound, G-sound, and K-sound.

A BREIEF INTRODUCTION TO NURSERY RHYMES

THE IMPORTANCE OF NURSERY RHYMES

There are several reasons why nursery rhymes are one of the best tools increasing success in reading and learning in children.

First and foremost, when they are properly performed, nursery rhymes are found to improve children of phonological awareness and fluency.

Secondly, nursery rhymes are one of the tools that when used correctly can increasing children's vocabulary and spelling.

Thirdly, nursery rhymes are known for developing communication skills. As kids recite nursery rhymes they learn to inflect their voices, to pause, to pitch their voices, and to increase the volumes of their voice to make meaning.

Fourthly, nursery rhymes are a good tool for introducing concepts to the kids. These concepts can be scientific concepts, mathematical concepts, or social concepts. For example some nursery rhymes have been used to introduce kids to concept such as counting, naming body parts and interdependence in an environment.

Fifthly, nursey rhymes also are known for sharpening children's crucial learning skills such as memorizing, recalling, anticipating, predicting, and following instruction.

Sixthly, nursery rhymes are also found to increase children's abilities to wait, take turns, and participating in collaborative activities.

SUKURI NIYO

Sukuri niyo,

Iti toto.

Gwagwe lo po ilo.

Ilo gwe'de merese kata.

'Ben do de jekaji, a woŋe di kuuk na kuuk.

Sukuri niyo.

Kiji koko.

Gwagwe lo po ilo.

Ilo gwe'de kayata kata.

'Ben do de jekaji, a woŋe di Kuuk na kuuk.

Sukuri niyo.

Lubi koko.

Gwagwe lo po ilo.

Ilo gwe'de kö'diyöt kata.

'Ben do de jekaji, a woŋe di kuuk na kuuk.

BÖNI BÖN KOTET

Waso, böni bön kotet.

Kukuli, tine ti mede.

Waso, böni bön kotet.

Kukuli, gane ga mede.

Waso, böni bön kotet.

Kukuli, rite rit mede.

Waso, böni bön kotet.

Kukuli, teŋe teŋ mukun.

Waso, böni bön kotet.

Kukuli, moke mok mukun.

Waso, böni böni kotet.

Kukuli, nyöni nyö mukun.

KURI WOMBOLIRO

Kuri, kuri,

Kuri womboliro,

Kuri, lo pi kuwen,

Kuri, do linda sokorok kwe.

Kuri, kuri,

Kuri womboliro,

Kuri, lojo kutuk,

Kuri, do linda sokorok kwe.

Kuri, kuri,

Kuri womboliro,

Kuri, lojo morin.

Kuri, do linda sokorok kwe.

KO LO JUWÖN

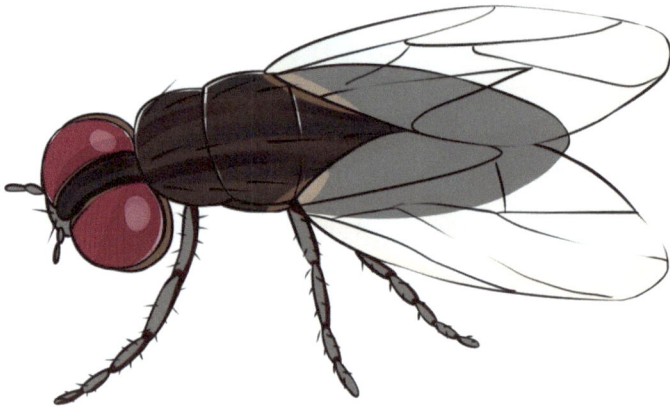

Ko lo juwön, ko lo juwön,
De köduŋöti lo deden.
Ko lo juwön, ko lo juwön,
De köduŋöti lo wuwulun.
Ko lo juwön, ko lo juwön,
De köduŋöti lo tutuk.
Ko lo juwön, ko lo juwön,
De köŋoti lo kekep.

DO KULYA DA?

Jukalu, do kulya da?

Nan kulya di,

Ɗine ki kak na waran.

Jukalu, do kulya da?

Nan kulya di,

Dumu kole kak na waran.

Jukalu, do kulya da?

Nan kulya di,

Dumu kere, kak na waran.

Jukalu, do kulya da?

Nan kulya di,

Dumu wale, kak na waran.

Jukalu, do kulya da?

Nan kulya di,

Dumu gor, kak na waran.

Jukalu, do kulya da?

Nan kulya di,

Kute kimaŋ, kak na waran.

NAN DE LWOK DO KO NYO?

Wur, kiki'dik, kiki'dik,

Koloŋ gwogwo,

Nan de mok do ko nyo?

Könin liyo tutu, mokot liyo lo geleŋ.

Wur, kiki'dik, kiki'dik,

Koloŋ gwogwo,

Nan de joŋ do ko nyo?

Könin liyo tutu, mokot liyo lo geleŋ.

Wur, kiki'dik, kiki'dik,

Koloŋ gwogwo,

Nan de lwök do ko nyo?

könin liyo tutu, mokot liyo lo geleŋ.

DO NYÖ KILO KINYO KWE KO NYO?

Lopoke, do nyö kilo kinyo kwe liŋ,
Gwak ko nyo?
Lopoke, do lin kilo kinyo kwe liŋ,
Gwak ko nyo?
Lopoke, do yek kilo kinyo kwe liŋ,
Gwak ko nyo?
Lopoke, do 'de kilo kinyo kwe liŋ,
Gwak ko nyo?
Lopoke, do kut kilo kinyo kwe liŋ,
Gwak ko nyo?

WUWA YEÐGI

Wuwa, wuwa,
Ko 'ben do doŋo kwe i kijo.
Wuwa, böŋö,
Ko 'ben doŋo kwe i kijo.
Wuwa, iti,
Ko 'ben doŋo kwe i kijo.
Wuwa, yeŋgi,
Ko 'ben doŋo kwe i kijo.

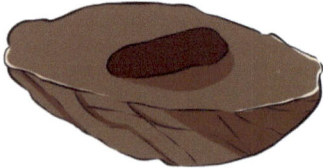

13

RINE RI MURUT

Logoro, rine ri mugun,

Ado do memet munu lo kinye.

Logoro, rine ri murut,

Ado do memet munu lo kinye.

Logoro, medi meda go,

Ado memet munu lo kinye.

Logoro, rumara rumara,

Ado momok munu lo kinye.

Logoro toyiŋgi toyiŋga,

Ado momok munu lo kinye.

Logoro, ŋane ŋa kutuk,

Ado momok munu lo kinye.

GWOJI GWOJA LONYUMEĐ

Nyesi nyesu, lonyumeŋ,

Đa lo konda do, lonyumeŋ?

Gwoji gwoja, lonyumeŋ.

Đa konda do, lonyumeŋ?

Biryöni biryö lonyumeŋ.

Đa lo konda do, lonyumeŋ?

Lyöŋi lyöŋön, lonyumeŋ.

Đa konda do, lonyumeŋ?

YARO YARO GWORLEK

Yaro, yaro, gworlek,

Kweki nan kala kulök.

Yaro, yaro, gworlek,

Kweki nan kume lelut.

Yaro, yaro gworlek,

Kweki nan kuwen kulök.

Yaro, yaro, gworlek,

Keweki nan suwö kulök.

Yaro, yaro, gworlek,

Kweki nan kotet nenut.

Yaro, yaro, gworlek,

Kweki nan mugun nenut.

LOTOME, LOTOME

Lotome, lotome,

Monye liyo liya?

Monye liyo twan.

Ɖa lo ryoga?

A do lo ryoga!

NAN SONYO KARE

Nan kaje sonyo kare.

Ko kudu kwe.

Ama nan koko pondi mede,

A nan ko tikini,

Köyikötöt, nagwon patata parik, parik.

Kune kulya kwe ti rurupe.

Diri 'depa ko ŋote lege

Na pömöni parik, parik,

Gwoso töri kwe i kuwe.

DÖMÖNÖŊ KO GORO

Dömönöŋ ko goro,

Dömönöŋ goro kayit,

Mu kunu goro kayaŋ,

ko baba kadi.

Dömönöŋ ko goro,

Dömönöŋ goro kayit,

Mu kunu goro kayaŋ,

Ko mama kadi.

Dömönöŋ ko goro,

Dömönöŋ goro kayit,

Munu kunu goro kayaŋ,

Ko mananye kadi.

LUGÖGÖRI LO KWE KI

Lugögöri lo kwe ki.

Warak, warak, kwe ki.

Lugögöri lo kwe murut.

Warak, warak, kwe murut.

Lugögöri lo kwe kidi.

Warak, warak, kwe kidi.

Lugögöri lo kwe mokot.

Warak, warak, kwe mokot.

Lugögöri lo kwe ki.

Ti nan gwak kondi ada?

Dumu koke kunö ki!

TA WIRYAN

Ta wiryan,

Ko lin ta lisörit kwe.

Koŋuti kunu,, kurju i luköbi,

Ilu kikwöti.

Ta wiryan,

Ko nyö ta lisorit kwe.

Koŋuti kunu,

Ko kinyo luköbi,

Ilu kikwoti.

Ta wiryan,

Ko yek ta lisörit kwe.

Koŋuti kunu,

A dukö luköbi,

Ilu kiwöti.

LO'DOKE, LO'DOKE

Lo'doke, lo'doke,

Köli kö mokot liyo.

Nan a köyu.

Ama kudu de?

Ama morogo na baba nu.

Ama moru kulu kata yu?

A nan de atu pokin lele suwöt.

Lo'doke, lo'doke,

Köli kö mokot liyo.

Nan a köyu.

Ama kudu de?

Ama morogo na baba nu.

Ama nyanyi kulu kata yu?

A nan de atikinda se kwe moyit kata.

RYAƊGAK LO PONDA

Gweŋgwe kurin!

Lo wori lo mama.

Ɗo lo ryaŋga,

Lo ponda mede.

Ilo de jambu kulya ti buröt.

Walele!

Ti likito lo nyömörö.

SISI NA KARE

Sisi, do meran ko piyoŋ,

Sisi na kare?

Sisi do na ko lodok,

Sisi na kare.

Sisi do meran ko piyoŋ,

Sisi na kare?

Sisi do na ko kulya,

Sisi na kare.

Sisi do meran ko piyoŋ,

Sisi na kare?

Sisi kodo ko kulya,

Sisi tuke tuk kulya.

LOGWULUKUK LOGWON DUMA

Kuruke ko widi,

Womboliro lo ko miji.

Ama nan Logwuluk logon duma,

Nan me'yu wele, gwololo kwe.

Logunu lo ko kuru,

Logoro lo ko munu.

Ama nan Logwuluk logwon duma,

Nan nyesu welet

Gwololo kwe.

WOWE GWOJI

Wowe medi,

Ama nan tin do miji lo kere.

Wowe pondi,

Ama nan tin do miji lo kere.

Wowe yiŋgi,

Ama nan tin do miji lo kere.

Wowe gwoji,

Ama nan tin do miji lo kere.

Wowe jambi,

Ama nan tin do miji lo kere.

TIKIN NA MUJIN

Kokan, kokan,

Ti nan mujin.

A nan tikin do,

Kune kwe, kune kwe.

Kokan, kokan,

Jaki nan mujin.

A nan tikin do,

Kune kwe, kune kwe.

KAPAYAK KUNE JONDA KUDU

Kapayak kayaŋ kune jonda kudu,

Kogwede kurilön, jonda kolöŋ.

Kapayak kayaŋ jonda lika,

Kogwede kurilön, jonda pape.

Kapayak kayaŋ kune jonda lyöŋön,

Kogwede kurilön, jonda yuran.

KOꞐA LO PURIYÖRÖ

Namanyaŋ, namanyaŋ,

Nan di koŋa lo puriyörö,

Namanyaŋ, namanyaŋ,

Nan di koŋa lo puriyörö,

Nan adi köli kö nan,

kogwon toto nabut na tetenda mugun na ŋutu.

Nan adi köli kö nan,

kogwon toto nabut na ririjö mugun na ŋutu.

Nan di köli kö nan,

kogwon toto nabut na kukunda mugun na ŋutu.

Nan adi köli kö nan,

kogwon toto nabut na to'bijoju mugun na ŋutu.

JIKI NAN BOLOK

Kapaparat, kapaparat,

Do nabut,

Jiki nan bolok,

Diloŋ niyo winyan.

Kapaparat, kapaparat,

Do nabut,

Jaki nan bolot,

Diloŋ niyo winyan.

KOKA LU LOGA

Ko kudu lo jön ko koloŋ to,
Koka lu loga.
Ko kudu lo jön ko koloŋ to,
Koka lu liba.
Ko kudu lo jön ko koloŋ to,
Koka lu tiju.
Ko kudu lo jon koloŋ to,
Koka lu kebu.

MIJI SIDA LOTEK

Yakulo,

Medi ta lu miji,

Lu miji sida lotek,

Lu miji totoyiŋga.

Yakulo,

medi ta lu miji

Lu miji sida lotek

Lu miji boboŋga.

Yakulo,

Medi ta lu miji,

Lu miji sida lotek,

Lu miji kekeja.

Yakulo,

Medi ta lu miji,

Lu miji sida lotek

Lu miji totokulyaju.

www.ingramcontent.com/pod-product-compliance
Lightning Source LLC
Chambersburg PA
CBHW042117040426
42449CB00002B/71